Christmas Wreaths
A Complete Guide to Make Your Own Wreaths

Copyright © 2020

All rights reserved.

DEDICATION

The author and publisher have provided this e-book to you for your personal use only. You may not make this e-book publicly available in any way. Copyright infringement is against the law. If you believe the copy of this e-book you are reading infringes on the author's copyright, please notify the publisher at: https://us.macmillan.com/piracy

Contents

Basic Fresh Christmas Wreath................1
Make a Christmas Ornament Wreath......9
Burlap Covered Wreath........................16
Classic Christmas Wreath Trio.............28
Honeycomb Christmas Wreath.............33
Simple Wire Wreath.............................38
White Winter Wreath...........................44
Joy Wreath Sign...................................52

Basic Fresh Christmas Wreath

The process is actually really simple and easy to do. If you have enough evergreen to work with, it's also very inexpensive.

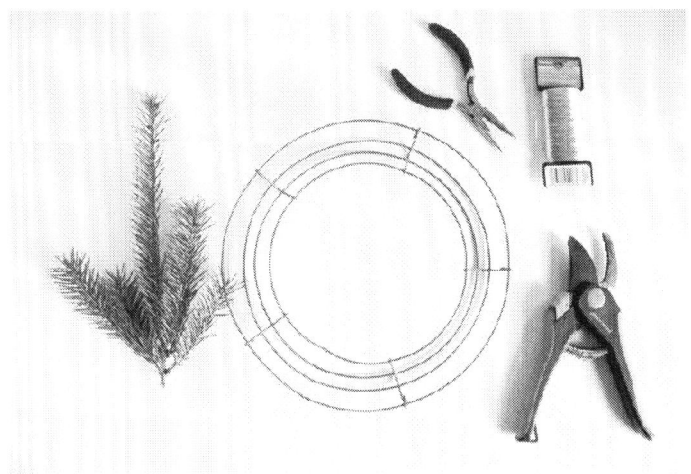

All you need is....

Wire wreath form

Floral wire

Gardening/pruning shears

Wire cutter

Optional: Embellishments and Battery Operated Lights

Material notes: You can pick up a wire wreath form for under

$2 at most craft or general stores and floral wire usually runs about the same price. Keep in mind that you do not necessarily need a large wreath form. I used a small wreath form for my wreath. It almost tripled in size because of the volume of the boughs. The floral wire will last you for about 2-3 wreaths, and the wire wreath form is reusable year after year, making this project super affordable and a great investment in future evergreen wreath making.

1. Cut 8-10 inch sprigs of evergreen needles and group them together into small bundles. The thicker your bundles, the thicker your wreath. Try to keep the sizes of the bundles

consistent, so that your wreath will be even.

2. Lay your first bundle, inside the concave groove of the wire wreath form. Wrap and twist floral wire around the base of the bundle and the wire wreath form about five times. Do not cut the wire yet.

3. Lay another bundle on top of the first bundle, staggering the spacing a couple of inches. Wrap floral wire around the base of the next bundle about 4-5 times.

4. Continue around the wreath, repeating step three.

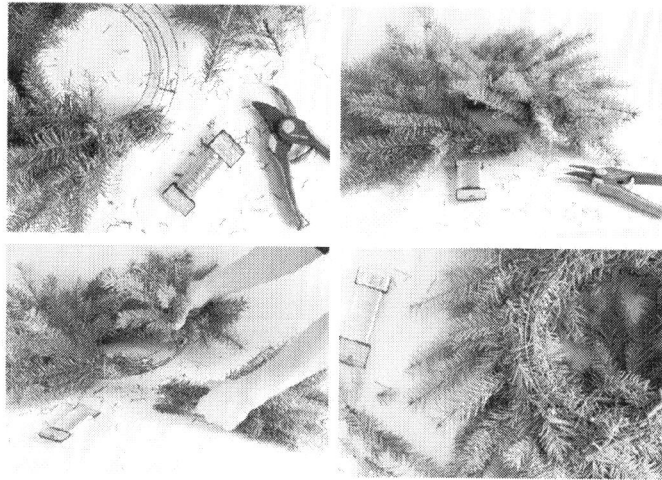

5. When you come around to where you started, simply lift up the top of the first bundle, and keep adding more bundles underneath it, until the wreath looks full and complete. Cut the wire and secure the cut end by twisting it to the wire wreath form.

6. Optional: Add embellishments, other varieties of evergreen and/ or some twinkle lights.

Christmas Wreaths

You can program the lights to stay on or flash on and off. They run off AA batteries, and they automatically shut off after 6 hours, so you can turn them on and then forget them. The lights are also woven into a flexible wire, so you can easily twist and secure the lights in place.

Christmas Wreaths

Make a Christmas Ornament Wreath

It's the most wonderful time of the year. And perhaps the craftiest time of the year, if you enjoy holiday projects. This quick and easy Christmas wreath is the perfect place to start decking your halls (or your front door).

You just need a few simple materials and it comes together quickly, so you can hang your creation in no time at all. You can also customize this wreath to look great with your existing holiday decor, no matter what you have. It looks great hanging on a door, on a wall, over a mantel, or just about anywhere.

Gather Your Materials

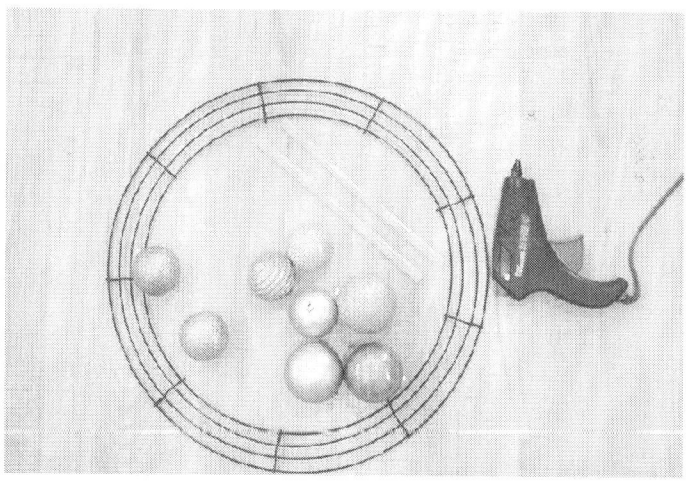

As you're choosing your ornaments to create the wreath, you'll most likely want to choose the shatterproof kind, which is made of a plastic material that still resembles the look of standard glass ornaments. It will make your wreath much more durable and you won't have to be concerned about breakage.

Tools and Supplies

- Wire wreath form
- Shatterproof (plastic) Christmas ornaments in various sizes
- Hot glue gun
- Glue sticks

Hot Glue Your Ornaments

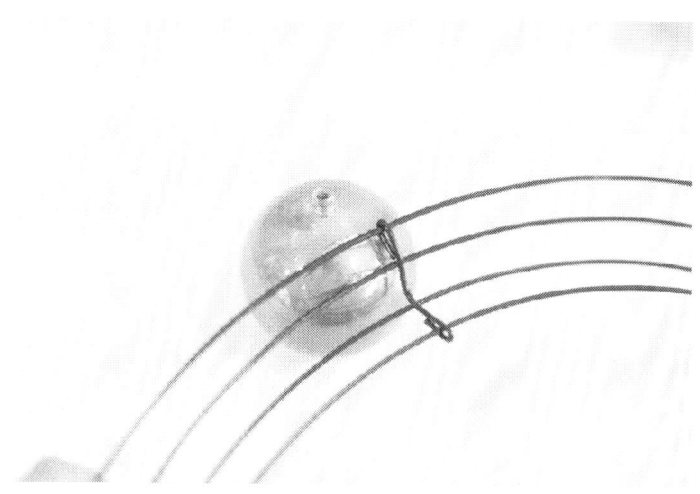

Start by hot gluing your first ornament onto the wreath form. For this first ornament, find a joint on the wreath form where a few wires come together. Place lines of glue on the top of the wires and quickly place the ornament on over the glue. Hold in place until set. We recommend using larger ornaments for this base layer.

Cluster Your Ornaments

Continue gluing in the same manner, beginning to make clusters with your ornaments. You may want to remove the ornament hangers from each ornament as you glue them on; this is up to your preference, but it might create more space for you to place your ornaments. We also recommend placing the ornaments on the wreath with the hanger side hidden, so that the smooth, round part of all the balls is what is displayed on the front of the wreath.

Continue Coverage

Christmas Wreaths

Keep gluing your ornaments to the wire wreath form. As you glue on your ornaments, begin not only gluing them to the form, but also to each other. The more points of contact that are glued together, the sturdier your wreath will be. It's best to try to glue an ornament to the wire and at least two additional points on other ornaments.

Complete the Layer

Complete coverage of your wire form with larger ornaments until you've reached the point where you started.

Add Another Layer

Use the same technique to add another layer of smaller ornaments over your first layer of large ornaments. You'll be mainly gluing the ornaments to each other for this layer because the wire wreath form should be mostly covered. As you are adding ornaments, take care to hide any wire that is showing with the smaller ornaments. You may need to nestle them into each other to get good coverage. Continue this layer until all wire is hidden.

Hang It Up

Hang your wreath on a sturdy hook. After it's hung, step back and ensure that the wires are hidden from all angles.

You may need to take it down and adjust. Once you're happy with the coverage, hang it back up and enjoy it all holiday season.

Burlap Covered Wreath

Supplies for wreath:

- Foam wreath form (mine said it was 12", but really it's about 15" with the width)
- 1.5 to 3 yards red burlap (my friend made a smaller 12" wreath with 1.5 yards, but I needed almost 3 yards to cover mine!)
- Circle die cut OR scissors and drinking glass
- Straight pins or hot glue gun
- Ribbon or fabric strip for hanging

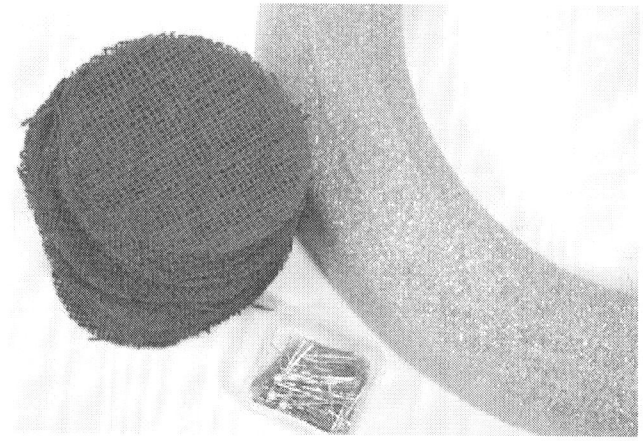

1. Cut your burlap into 3" circles. I used my Sizzix Big Shot and a 3" circle die cut. You could also trace a drinking glass

and cut by hand with scissors.

2. Fold each circle in half, then in half again. Pin or hot glue to wreath. Tip: If you're using flat head pins (which are waaay cheaper), try to insert pin into a strand of the burlap instead of between holes--it will help it stay in place!

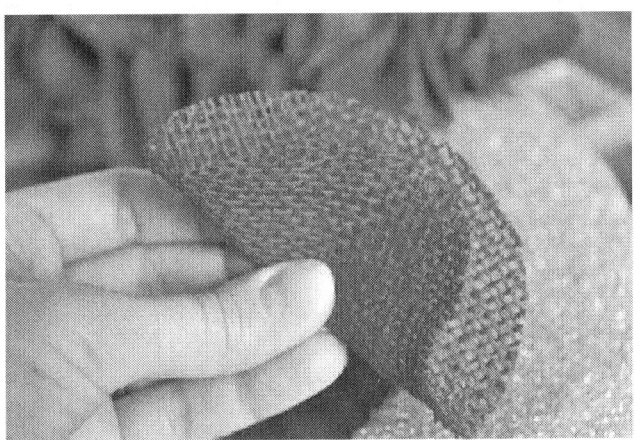

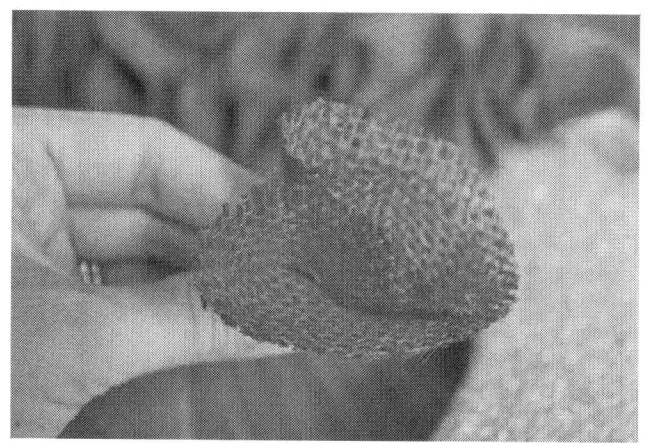

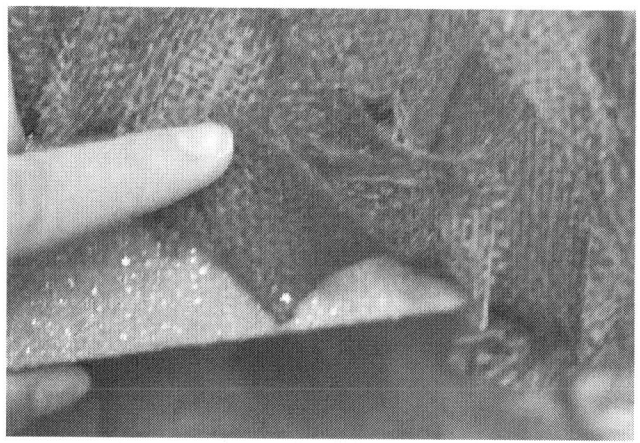

Continue pinning, turning petals in different direction to make it fuller. Be sure to cover the inside and outside of wreath as well. Leave the back bare.

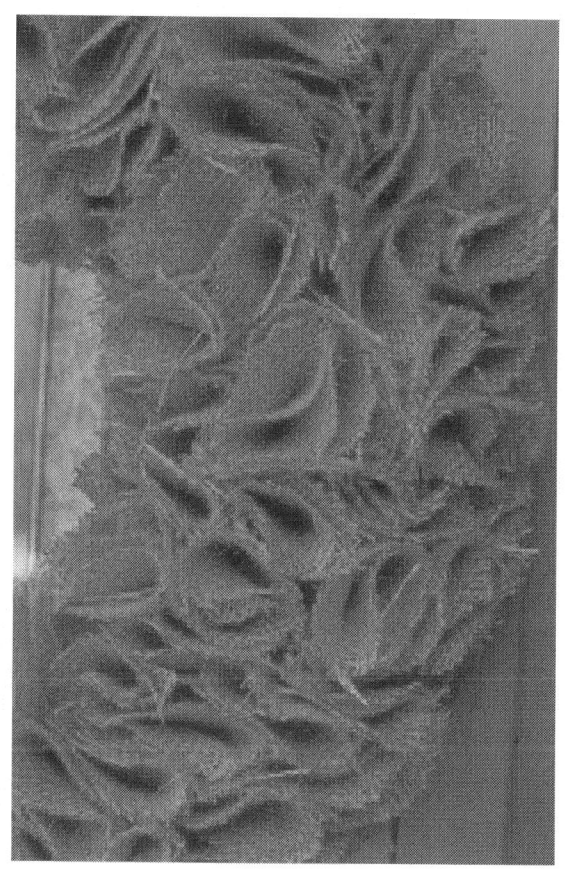

When it's full, you're done! Hang with a piece of ribbon or fabric

If you want to add a little kick, add a simple stick star to your wreath. Here's how:

Paper Covered Stick Star Tutorial

Supples:

- Dry sticks from your yard or the local park
- Sheet music or other paper
- Paper cutter
- Hot glue gun
- Jute, twine, yarn, or string to match
- Berries and greenery (optional)

Christmas Wreaths

1. I originally painted my sticks white, but then I decided I wanted to use sheet music (to go with the theme of the rest of my decor). You decide what works best for your home. If you're using paper, cut it into approx. 1" strips with a paper cutter.

2. Starting at one end, begin wrapping the strips around each stick, hot gluing here and there along the way. Add strips until entire stick is covered.

If you run into bumps, just press the paper over the bump and make a hole in it. It really doesn't have to be perfect!

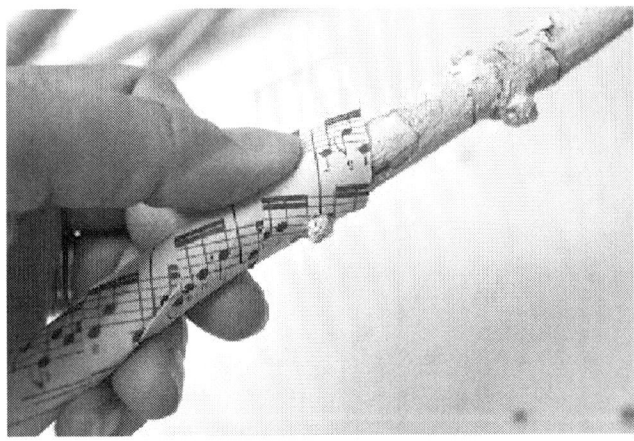

3. When all your sticks are covered, arrange them in a star shape, slightly overlapping sticks. Hot glue sticks together at intersecting points.

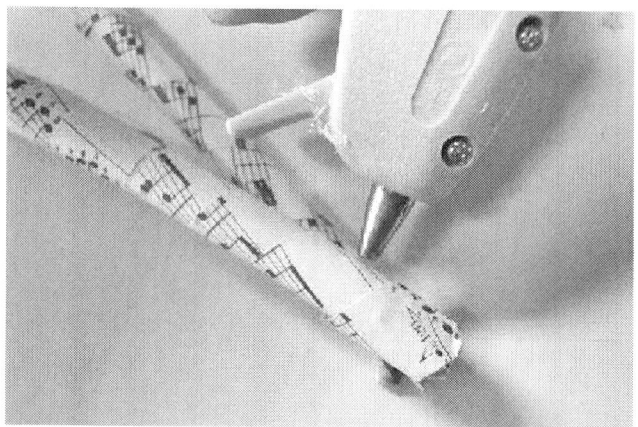

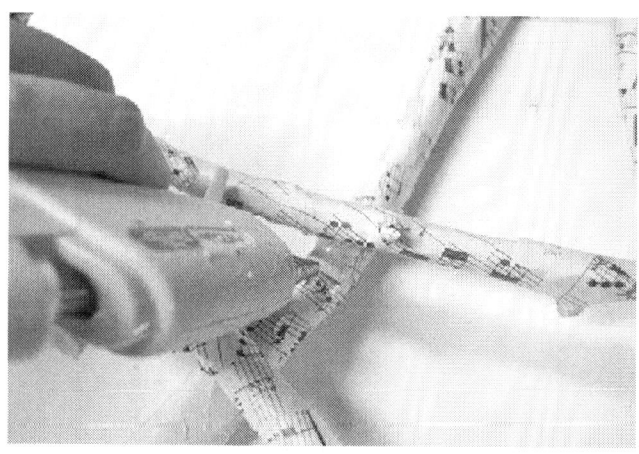

4. Tie each of the 5 points together with a piece of jute, yarn, or string to give it a little more stability (plus it's cuter!)

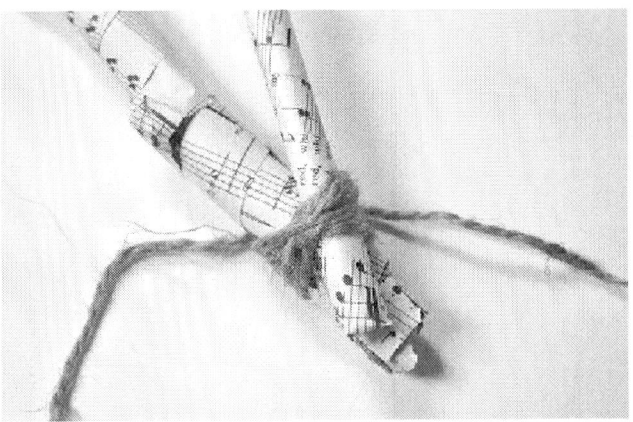

5. Tie a bunch of greenery (I cut mine from a bush in my

yard) and berries (I used fake because the berries in my yard are purple!) to the top point of the star.

Hang over the top of your wreath, or alone if you want! That's it!

Classic Christmas Wreath Trio

Materials:

Boxwood Wreath with Berries

Aluminum Hobby Wire

Red Velvet Ribbon

Step One. Use wire to attach all three wreaths together.

Christmas Wreaths

Step Two. Cut a strip of the velvet ribbon to fit around wreaths. Secure by tying in the back or with some strong double-sided tape.

Christmas Wreaths

Step Three. Create a bow and thread a small piece of wire through the back to attach to wreath.

Holiday Cheer

All that's left to do is hang your trio on your front door to greet all your holiday guests!

Honeycomb Christmas Wreath

Materials needed: 16" diameter styrofoam wreath form,

honeycomb palm tree picks, scissors, straight pins, green crepe paper streamer, assorted honeycomb balls in green, reds and pinks

Christmas Wreaths

38

Step 1: Begin by covering the wreath form with green crepe paper. Secure with straight pins.

Step 2: Assemble the palm tree picks, honeycomb balls, and fans. Experiment with cutting different shapes and size balls and fans.

Step 3: Create 'trees' by stacking three palm tree picks. While the paper is flat, trim the tissue paper to create the middle and top of the tree.

Step 4: Being sticking the trees into the floral wreath. You may have to cut the ends of the toothpicks so they don't poke out the backside.

Step 5: Using straight pins, begin securing the red and pink honeycomb decorations. Use a random mix for variety. There's no right or wrong way to do this step – just fill up the wreath!

Step 6: Add a ribbon loop on the back for hanging. Alternately, you could loop a ribbon through the wreath to hang.

Step 7: Optional: add a written "banner" to say Happy

Holidays, Season's Greetings or Bah Humbug, whatever you heart desires!

Christmas Wreaths

Simple Wire Wreath

Materials

- Wire wreath frames, i used a 12" frame & 18" frame
- Metallic gold interior/exterior spray paint for metal surfaces
- Hot glue gun and glue sticks
- Faux greenery stems (i grabbed mine from hobby lobby, no idea what type of leaf they are!)
- Clear adhesive hooks

Christmas Wreaths

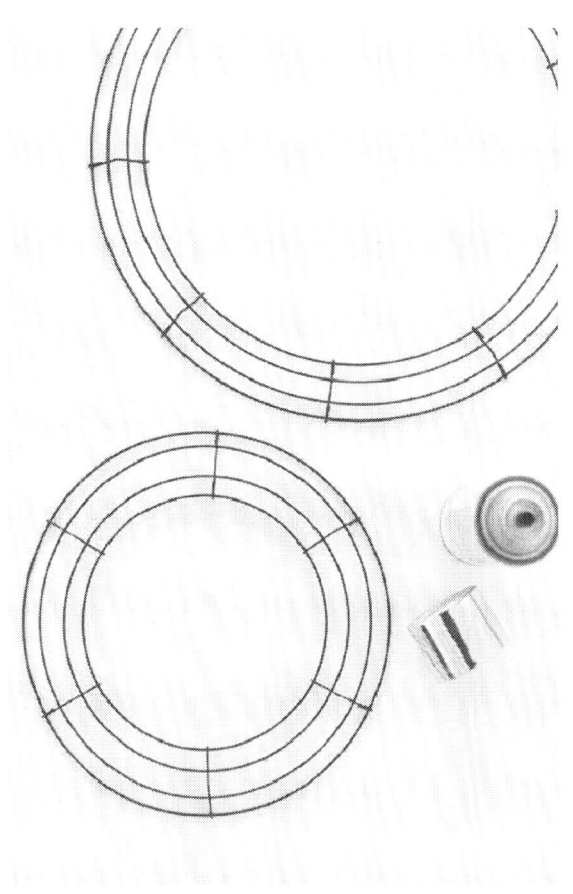

Christmas Wreaths

These project is two easy steps: first, spray paint the wire frames gold and let them dry. Second, hot glue your greenery on, then hang with clear adhesive hooks!

Pretty simple, right?! The options are pretty much endless on the shapes and sizes of the wire frames since they sell so many kinds for crafting.

White Winter Wreath

Materials and Tools Needed:

- power drill or awl tool (the awl tool might be tricky/dangerous)
- metal pliers
- white florist wire
- white florist tape
- coat hanger (the flimsier the better)
- artificial baby's breath or similar whispy flower
- white ping pong balls (I used 17)
- 2/3 yard of wide ribbon
- scissors
- optional: hot glue gun

Step One: Using the metal pliers, pull apart the twisted neck of the wire hanger. Use the pliers to bend out any kinks in the wire and to shape it into a circle. You don't have to worry about getting out all of the kinks around the neck of the hanger, because they are helpful in twisting together the ends again after you've made the circle. The reattachment point doesn't need to be perfect—just cover it with the bulkiest portion of flowers during the next step.

Step Two: Cut the stems off the baby's breath and portion each bunch into smaller segments. Starting at the top of the wreath, tape the pieces of baby's breath onto the wire frame. If your wire frame isn't white, you should wrap the wire with the white florist tape before adding the flowers. Florist tape only sticks to itself and it sticks the best when you pull on it as you wrap.

If you're concerned about the placement of the flower pieces, it may be helpful to lay them out before beginning, and maybe snap a quick picture to remember where the general placement should be. To keep your wreath asymmetrical like mine, build out the right side more than the left side of the wreath.

Step 3: After you've built the base of your wreath with the baby's breath taped to the wire frame, it's time to add the white balls. If you are hanging your wreath in a window or somewhere where it will be seen from behind, you might want to prep the ping pong balls by placing them in an empty egg carton, logo-side up, and spraying them with a coat of matte white spray paint.

After you've drilled or punched two holes in each ping pong ball, make a hook with the end of a 9" piece of wire and thread the wire through a ping pong ball. Attach the ball to the wire frame of the wreath, wrapping the excess wire a few times around, and then trimming the remaining portion with the metal pliers. To build a grouping of ping pong balls on your wreath, you may need to drill extra holes on the sides of the balls to thread wire through in order to connect the balls together.

Christmas Wreaths

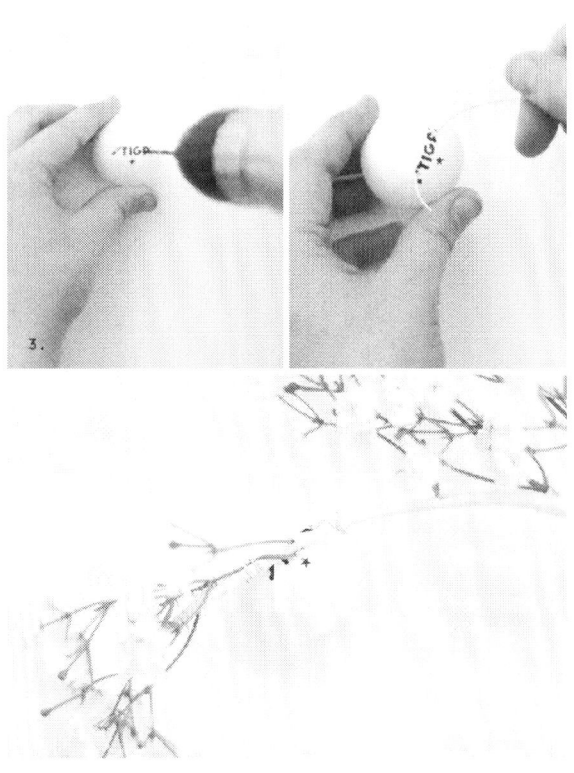

Christmas Wreaths

55

Christmas Wreaths

Joy Wreath Sign

Materials: 5 1×6" pine boards, 2 smaller 1" pine boards, paint, "Joy template," drill, 1/8" drill bit, 1/4" drill bit, Winslow Fir Garland, 22-gauge wire, 22" Gold Wreath with Berries, MSL Micro lights (optional)

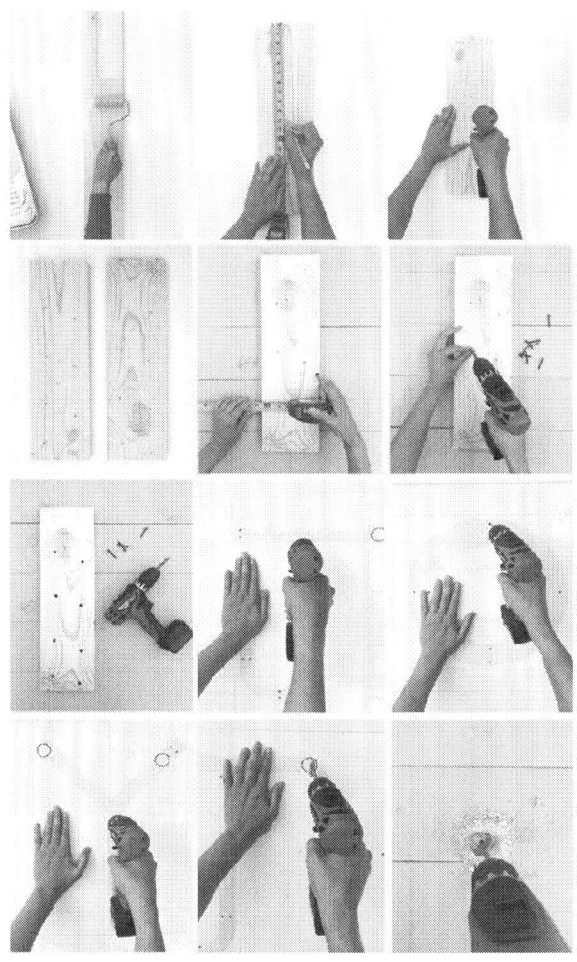

Step 1: Paint all of your pine boards to match the wall you are going to hang the sign on. Lay the 5 long boards side by

side (long side), creating a panel. Place the 2 shorter boards across the five on either end. Screw them in 11 1/2 inches from the ends.

Step 2: Place the "Joy" template on the front of the panel. Use a 1/8in drill bit to drill holes in the corresponding circles on the template, through the paper and panel. These allow you to wire the garland and wreath in place. Use a 1 1/4in bit to do the same with the larger corresponding holes in the template. Drill through the paper and panel. These holes are for the electric wires and garland.

Step 3: Unscrew and remove the top board and place the garland in the large holes, leaving 42in hanging at the front left for the J and 36in hanging at the front right for the Y. Reattach the top board.

Step 4: Following the arrows on the template, place the garland along the holes to create a J and a Y. Feed a 12in piece of 22-gauge wire through the holes and around the garland. Twist the loose ends underneath the panel to secure. Thread the electrical plug through the large hole, as

shown on the template. Fluff the garland.

Step 6: Place the wreath on the center of the board. Feed a 12in piece of 22-gauge wire through the indicated holes around the top of the wreath and through to the back. Twist the loose ends underneath the panel to secure. Repeat at the bottom and on either side.

Step 6:Plug in to illuminate the garland. If you'd like to light all three letters, add microlights to the wreath!

Christmas Wreaths

Printed in Great Britain
by Amazon